What Was It Before It Got Wet?

by Kristen McCurry

PEBBLE
a capstone imprint

What do you think these things were
before they got wet?

Take a guess,
then turn each page to find out!

What was it?

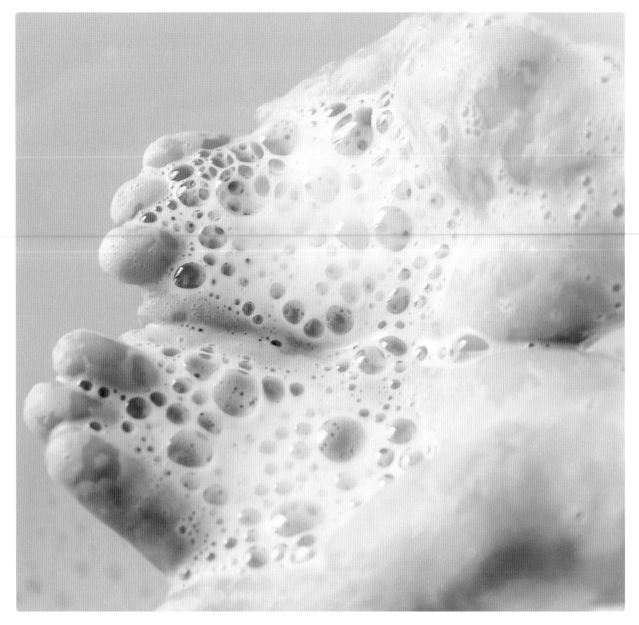

⇨ turn to see

A bar of soap.

Soap makes

bubbles

when it gets wet!

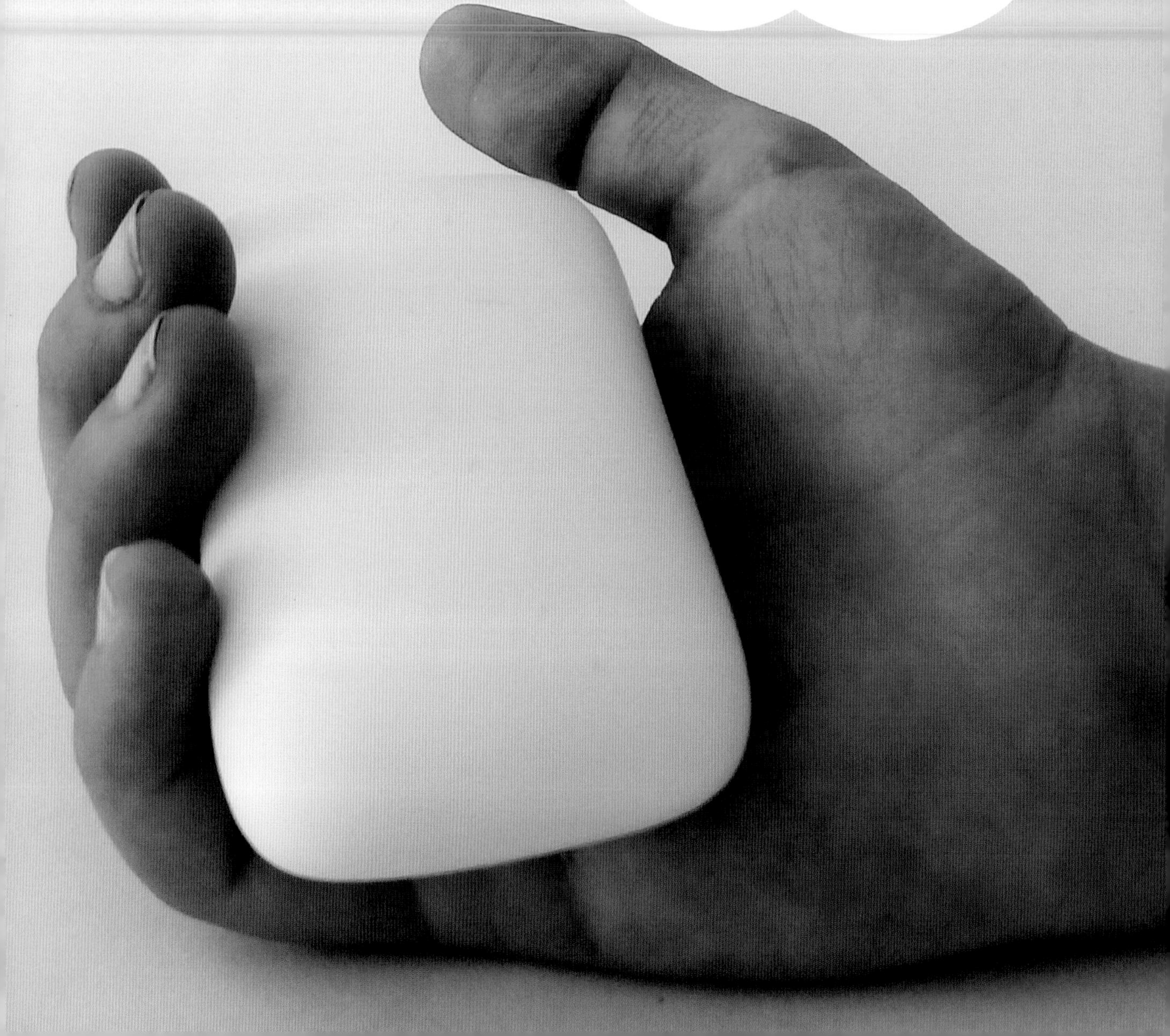

What was it?

⇨ turn
to see

Cocoa powder.

Mixing cocoa powder and hot water makes hot chocolate!

What was it?

⇨ turn to see

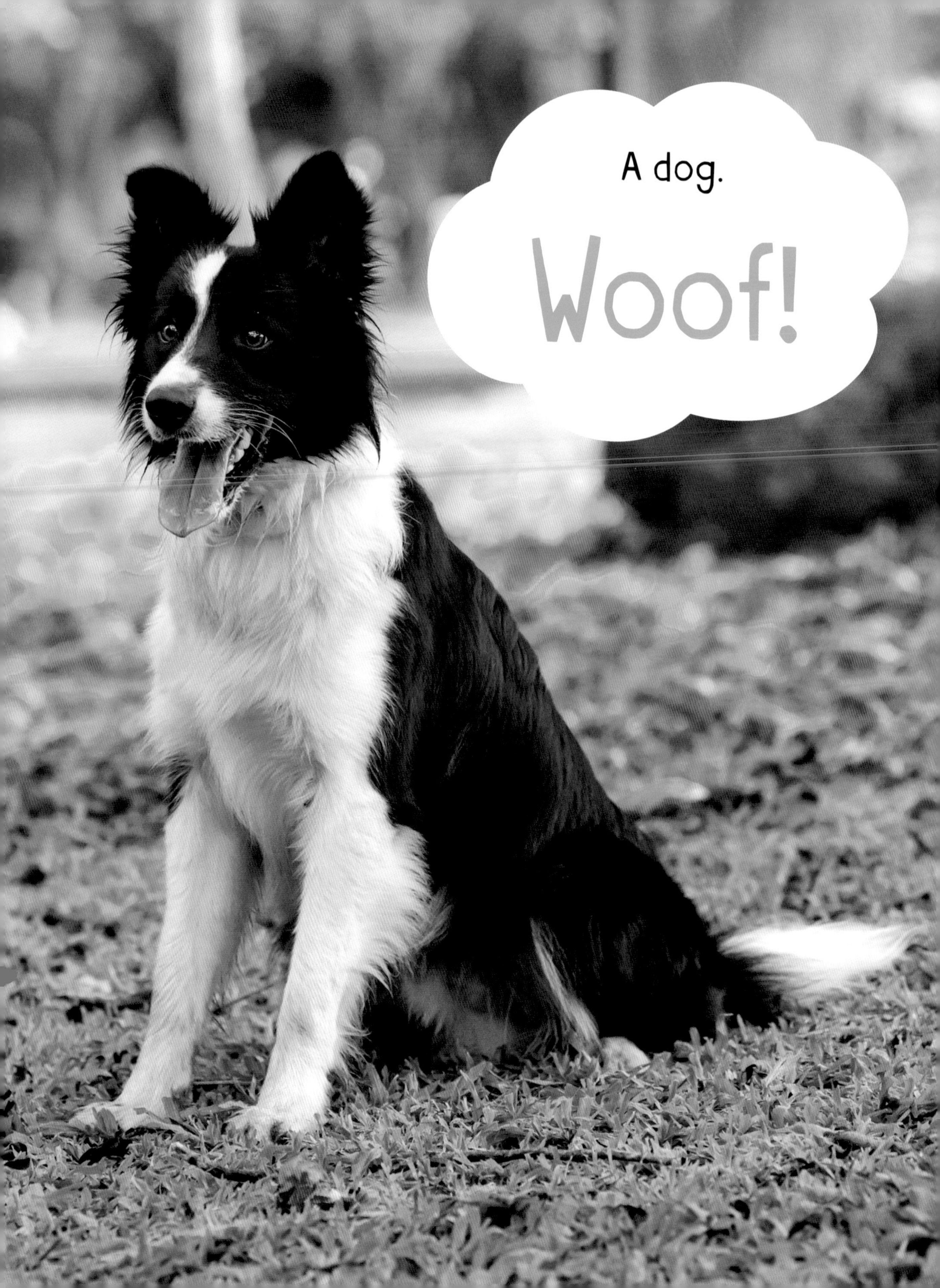

A dog.

Woof!

What was it?

turn
to see

A paint set.

What do you like to create
with watercolor paints?

What was it?

⇨ turn
to see

A dandelion.

Blow the seeds
and make a

wish!

What was it?

⇨ turn
to see

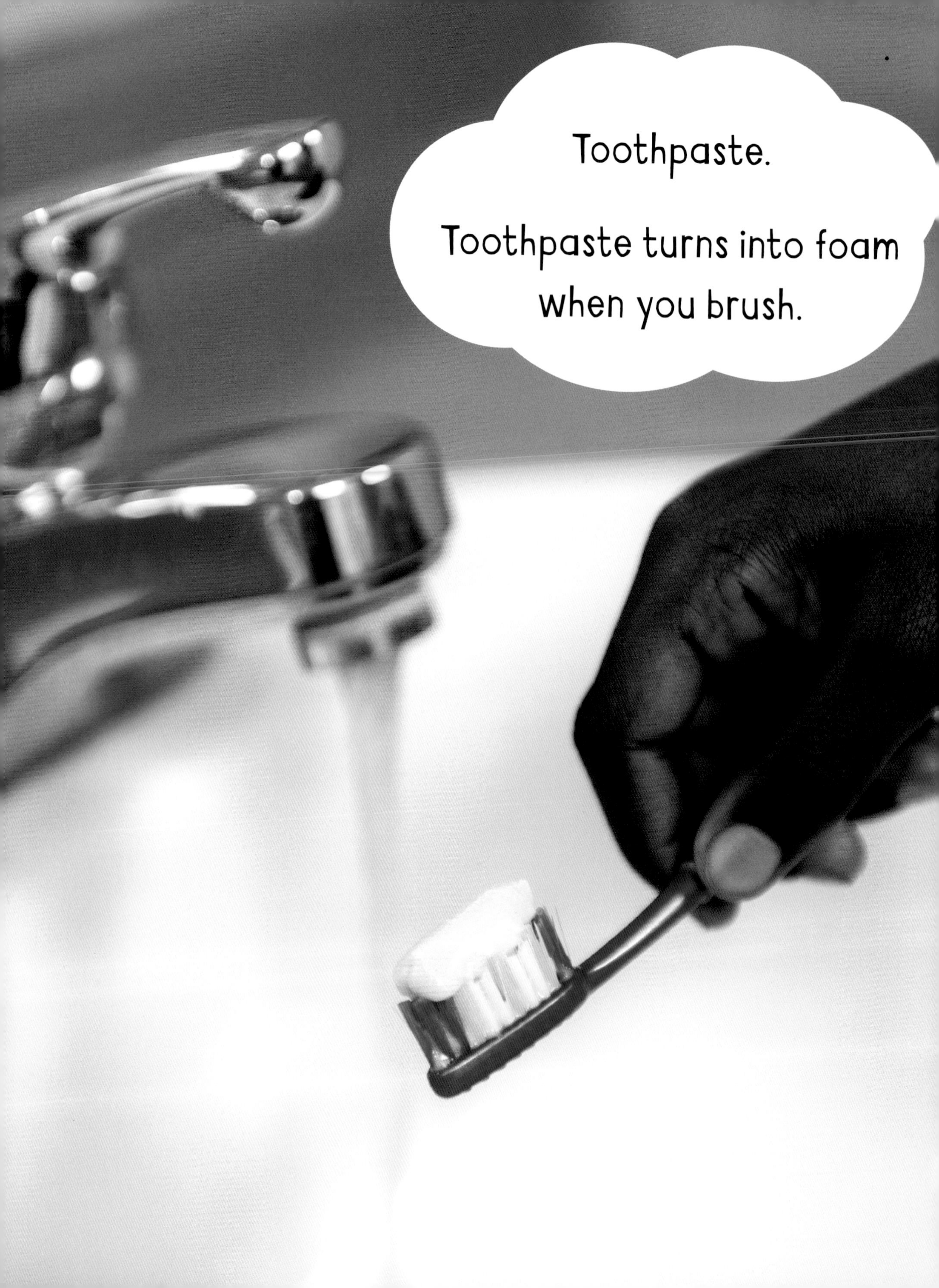

Toothpaste.

Toothpaste turns into foam when you brush.

What was it?

⇨ turn
to see

Dirt.

Water and dirt make mud.

Squish!

What was it?

turn
to see

Dry spaghetti noodles.

Cooking noodles in water makes spaghetti.

What was it?

turn to see

A sandcastle.

Waves

wash sandcastles away.

What was it?

⇨ turn
to see

What was it?

⇨ turn
to see

Did you guess a crocodile?

What was it?

⇨ turn
to see

A seed.

Water and sunlight help seeds grow into plants.

What was it?

⇨ turn
to see

A desert.

Even deserts
get wet from rain.

What was it?

⇨ turn
to see

A cute, fuzzy

koala!

Good job! Try all the books in this series!

What Was It Before It Was Smashed?
by Kristen McCurry
A turn-and-see book ➾

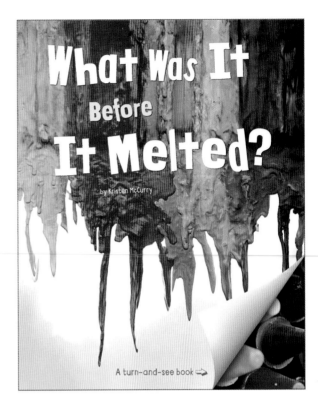

What Was It Before It Melted?
by Kristen McCurry
A turn-and-see book ➾

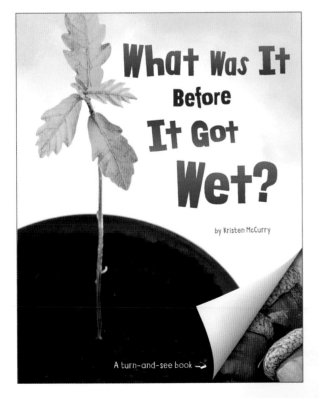

What Was It Before It Got Wet?
by Kristen McCurry
A turn-and-see book ➾

What Was It Before It Was Cut?
by Kristen McCurry
A turn-and-see book ➾

Pebble Sprout is published by Pebble, an imprint of Capstone.
1710 Roe Crest Drive
North Mankato, Minnesota 56003
www.capstonepub.com

Library of Congress Cataloging-in-Publication Data is available on the Library of Congress website.
ISBN 978-1-9771-1334-4 (hardcover)
ISBN 978-1-9771-2016-8 (paperback)
ISBN 978-1-9771-1338-2 (eBook PDF)
Summary: Splash! This photo-guessing game challenges pre-readers to guess what something was before it got wet. The soggy, soaked, and squishy answers may be surprising!

Designer: Sarah Bennett
Media Researcher: Eric Gohl
Production Specialist: Tori Abraham

Image credits
Capstone Studio: Karon Dubke, 13, 14, 18; iStockphoto: HaiGala, 19; Shutterstock: 2630ben, 23, Al Rublinetsky, 20, Alex Cofaru, 26, anna.q, 6, BB2, 16, Clayton Harrison, 27, Elayne Massaini, 8, FeSeven, 7, Gajus, 15, Gx.san, 11, ikadebah, 17, Ivana Jankovic, cover (bottom right), Ken Griffiths, 30, kornnphoto, 5, leelord, 24, Madlen, cover, makieni, 3, mars-design, 4, motorolka, 25, Patai Wonganutrohd, 9, Pina Suthaphan, 22, Pix One, 21, romantitov, 1, Shutova Elena, 12, twogiraffe, 28, Yulia YasPe, 10; SuperStock: Biosphoto, 29

Design Elements: Shutterstock

Printed in China.
002489